BEAR
TO THE
RESCUE

For all the very good dogs and their people who work together to protect our world. And for anyone who's ever felt like they're not enough, or been made to feel like they're too much – you're actually just right. – RC and NG

To all those who care for our world. And especially to my Nanna and Pop: Dorothy and Joe. – SM

© Text Romane Cristescu and Nic Gill 2025
© Illustrations Sylvia Morris 2025

A catalogue record for this book is available from the National Library of Australia

ISBN: 9781486314904 (hbk)
ISBN: 9781486321575 (pbk)
ISBN: 9781486314911 (epdf)
ISBN: 9781486321230 (epub)

Published by:
CSIRO Publishing
36 Gardiner Road, Clayton VIC 3168
Private Bag 10, Clayton South VIC 3169
Australia

Telephone: +61 3 9545 8400
Email: publishing.sales@csiro.au
Website: www.publish.csiro.au
Sign up to our email alerts: publish.csiro.au/earlyalert

Edited by Belinda Bolliger
Cover, text design and layout by Emilia Toia
Printed by Ingram Lightning Source

CSIRO acknowledges the Traditional Owners of the lands that we live and work on across Australia and pays its respect to Elders past and present. CSIRO recognises that Aboriginal and Torres Strait Islander peoples have made and will continue to make extraordinary contributions to all aspects of Australian life including culture, economy and science. The use of Western science in this publication should not be interpreted as diminishing the knowledge of plants, animals and environment from Indigenous ecological knowledge systems.

Note for teachers: Teacher notes are available at: https://www.publish.csiro.au/book/8024/#forteachers

BEAR
TO THE
RESCUE

ROMANE CRISTESCU
AND NIC GILL

ILLUSTRATED BY
SYLVIA MORRIS

CSIRO
PUBLISHING

Has anyone ever told you
you're too much?

Too loud?

Too annoying?

Too intense?

TOO MUCH!

People used to tell me that.

My name is Bear.

When I was a puppy,
people thought I was adorable.

It's true.
I *was* adorable.

But I'm also a working dog – that means I'm

FULL OF ENERGY.

I need to keep busy all day long!

In my first home, I wasn't given any jobs to do.

So, I had to make up my own.

I was **Bear: Shoe Finder.**

Bear: Interior Designer.

Bear: Renovator.

I took my work very seriously.
But no one seemed to appreciate it.

It was the same in my next home. And the next.
I stayed with a lot of different people, but none
of them knew what to do with me.

They called me naughty.
They said I was a bad dog.

'Bear, you're **TOO MUCH!**'

But one day, someone said something different.

'He's not bad.
He just needs a job.'

My new home was full of other dogs who
were a bit too much – just like me!

Maya, Billie and Baxter were working dogs too,
but they had really important jobs.

KOALA HABITAT

They spent their days helping researchers find koalas so they could study and protect them.

That sounded like something I could do.

I started training every day.
I began by looking for koala fur in the backyard.

Whenever I found it, I got a reward!

'Good boy Bear-Bear!'

I loved my new home and friends. I loved playing games.
And I loved sniffing out koala smells.

One day, I was ready.

'Hop in, Bear!'

The forest was even better than the backyard.
There were lots of interesting smells.

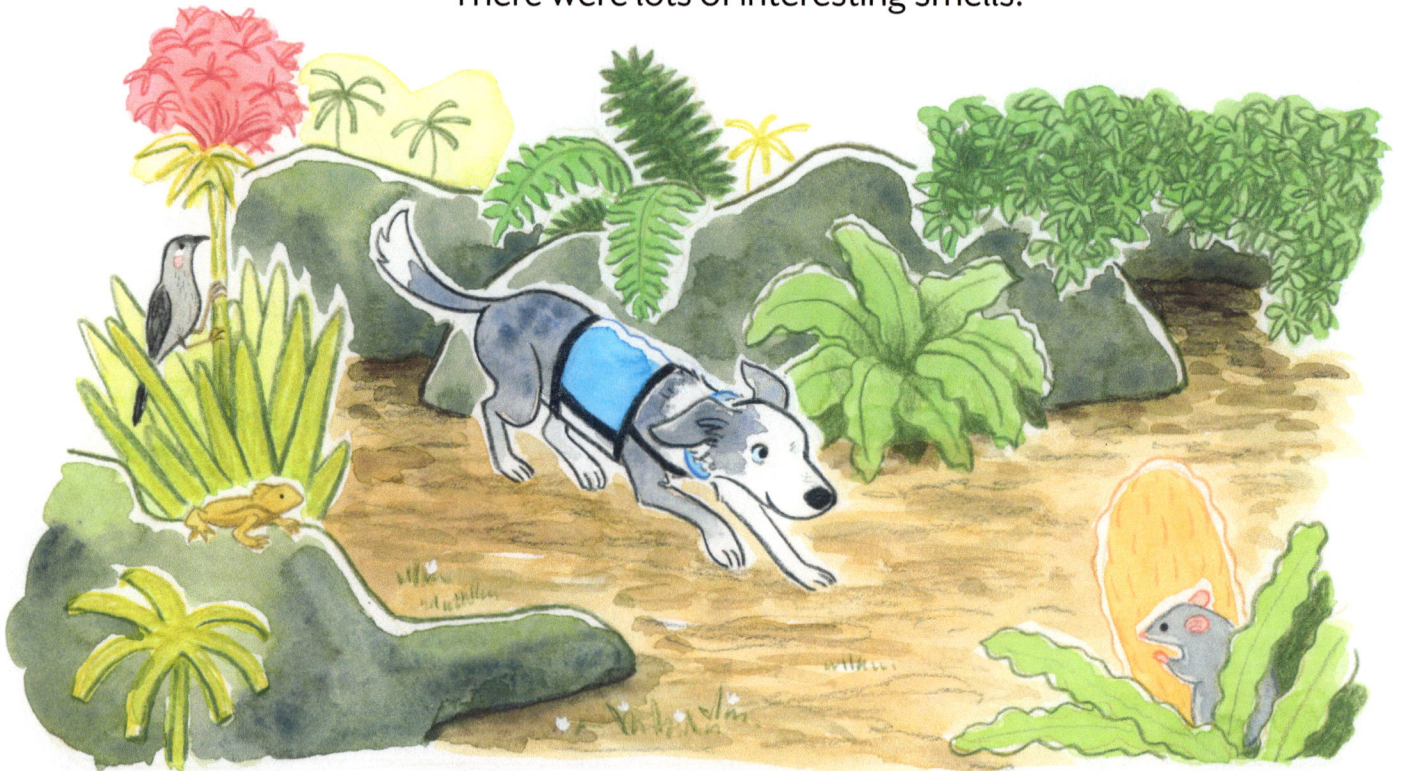

But there was only one smell
I was really interested in.

Then the fires came
and everything changed.

It was so quiet.

There were no more leaves.
There were no more grasses.
There were only ashes.

Where had all the animals gone?

Now I wasn't just looking for koalas to study them.
I had to find them to save them!

'Go find!'

This wasn't like working in the forests at home.
The air dried my nose and stung my eyes.

I wore special boots
to protect my paws.

The days were long and the work was hard.
Everyone around me looked sad and tired.

But they always smiled
when they saw me.

I tried my best to find the koalas.

Some were taken to special wildlife carers.
The carers bandaged the koalas' burns and made sure
they had enough to eat and drink.

HELP for WILDLIFE

When they were strong enough, the koalas were returned to their bushland homes.

Eventually, it was time for me to go home too.
This time, I hadn't been too much.

Everyone said I had been

too brave,

too clever,

too wonderful!

I hadn't just helped the koalas who'd been caught in the bushfires,

I had helped the people too.

I was now **Bear: Koala Conservation Dog.**

And finally, I was home.

THE STORY OF BEAR

(by Romane, one of Bear's humans)

The story of Bear really starts with the story of the koalas.

These beautiful Australian animals are in a lot of trouble. They face threats from the loss of their habitat, drought, heatwaves, and more recently, huge bushfires known as megafires, all of which have been made worse by climate change. Since I started working with koalas in 2006, I've watched their struggle.

Koalas can be difficult to study because of how hard it can be to find them. That's where conservation detection dogs can help. Dogs explore the world through their noses – what may be difficult for humans to see can sometimes be much easier to smell. Imagine a chocolate cake baking in the oven: you smell it before you see it!

I had an idea: maybe we could find koalas by sniffing out their poo. Focusing on poo may seem strange, but animal poo (called scats) and other animal traces, like feathers, paw prints or tracks, have long been used by human hunters. Now, ecologists – scientists who study nature – use these same signs to help find and protect wild animals and their habitats. Wherever there is koala poo, there is a koala making the poo! So, finding the poo helps us map where koalas live. For obvious (smelly) reasons, one of the best ways to look for poo is by smell. And who's great at smelling things? Dogs!

My first detection dog teammate was Maya, a koala-poo detection dog. When Maya finds poo, she drops to the ground and is rewarded by a play with her ball – her favourite thing in the world! Then I get to do *my* favourite thing – discovering where koalas are living so we can better understand and protect them. Maya and I started working at the University of the Sunshine Coast in Queensland, setting up the Detection Dogs for Conservation research team.

While I was working on koala poo sniffing, I met an amazing detection dog – Oscar the black Labrador – and his best mate, ecologist Dr Jim Shields. Rather than poo, Oscar was trained to sniff out live koalas. This was a great idea because sometimes, especially when a koala is in trouble, we need to find the koala itself and not just where it lives.

We started to search for the perfect live-koala detection dog, with help from the International Fund for Animal Welfare. And that's how we found Bear. Bear is an Australian Koolie, a working dog breed that often comes with what dog trainers call 'high drive' – which means they need a job to focus their energy. Bear was a very cute puppy, but as he grew older, he became increasingly mischievous. His boredom led to destructive behaviours and he was being passed on from one family to another.

Bear's latest family was getting desperate. When they heard our team was looking for a koala-dog trainee, it sounded like a perfect opportunity. What made Bear challenging in a home situation – his intensity, energy and playfulness – was just what was needed to become a successful conservation detection dog.

Bear came to us in 2017. After a rocky start to life, he had to learn how to trust and interact with humans, to become more confident and, perhaps most importantly, how to relax and live his best life! He went through a lot of training with us. We played all sorts of games with him, linking the smell of a live koala to opportunities for play. Finding a koala meant getting a ball! Because koalas live high up in trees, they are harder to find than koala poo, so Bear needed much more training than any of the other dogs in our team.

When he was ready, Bear started helping with koala rescue work. To begin with, he helped find sick koalas so that wildlife rescue groups could take them to vets for treatment. He also assisted with koala research work by finding koalas for the researchers to monitor.

Then the Black Summer of 2019–2020 arrived. Over a few months, huge bushfires burned through millions of hectares of the Australian landscape. These megafires shocked the world and were the largest fires ever recorded on the Australian continent. Amid the despair and destruction, I decided we needed to help.

Bear and his support team went wherever we were invited to lend a hand or a paw. We landed at Two Thumbs Wildlife Sanctuary in the New South Wales Snowy Mountains, which had been devastated by the fires, and spent many weeks searching for koalas. (The name 'Two Thumbs' comes from a unique feature of koalas' front paws – they have two digits that act like thumbs, which help them to climb.)

One of the koalas that Bear had found was Jessie, a four-year-old female. Jessie was so undernourished that the vet didn't think she would survive – the trees she relied upon for food and shelter had been stripped bare by fire. Jessie was carrying a female joey (a baby koala), who we named Amelia. If Jessie hadn't been found by Bear, it's likely neither mother nor baby would have survived.

We were delighted to save two koalas, but Jessie had a surprise for us. Shortly after being rescued, Jessie gave birth again – she'd been looking after not one baby, but two! We named the new joey Jazza, and when the trees had recovered enough to feed and protect them from the elements, all three koalas were released back into the Two Thumbs Wildlife Sanctuary.

Bear's work made a huge difference to the koalas at Two Thumbs. But sadly, the ongoing threats of habitat loss and climate change mean that Bear and his teammates need to keep working to help this beloved species, as well as other threatened species like quolls, greater gliders and even masked owls. In recognition of his work, Bear has received an International Fund for Animal Welfare Animal Action Award (2021) and the Puppy Tales Australian Dog of the Year Awards 'All Rescues Are Special' Medal (2025). Despite his many awards, Bear is still happy to sniff alongside other conservation detection dogs, scientists, wildlife rescuers and carers, working to protect our environment into the future.

Common name	Bear	Koala
Scientific name	*Canis familiaris*	*Phascolarctos cinereus*
Height	55 centimetres	68 to 82 centimetres
Weight	21 kilograms	5 to 8 kilograms
Features	Blue eyes	Fluffy ears, round head, sharp claws
Colour	Black, grey and white	Ash-grey fur, white chest (except adult males who have a brown patch from their scent gland)
Habitat	Comfy dog bed	Eucalypt forest
Favourite food	Pizza (but also a fan of chicken and sardines)	Eucalypt leaves
Favourite activity	Finding koalas … and chasing balls	Sleeping … and eating

Koalas have unique fingerprints, just like humans.

Dogs can detect *anything* that has a smell. Sniffer dogs have been trained to find endangered species, invasive animals, invasive plants, animal scats (poo), bird reject pellets (castings) and nests.

Koala poos are called pellets, and each koala produces about 100 pellets or more every day!

DID YOU KNOW?

Male koalas lie about their size: their bellow (the call they make during breeding season) is so low and powerful that they sound like they could be the size of a buffalo!

A dog's nose is estimated to be 100,000 to 100 million times more sensitive than a human nose (depending on the dog breed).

Koala poo is brown to green in colour, and small – between the size of an olive pit and an almond. It's also probably the best-smelling poo in the bush, thanks to the koalas' eucalypt leaf diet.

www.ingramcontent.com/pod-product-compliance
Lightning Source LLC
Chambersburg PA
CBHW042011080426
42734CB00002B/48